I0461756

Congressional
Research
Service

Housing for Persons Living with HIV/AIDS

Libby Perl
Specialist in Housing Policy

July 3, 2012

Congressional Research Service

7-5700

www.crs.gov

RL34318

CRS Report for Congress
Prepared for Members and Committees of Congress

Summary

Since the beginning of the acquired immunodeficiency syndrome (AIDS) epidemic in the early 1980s, many individuals living with the disease have had difficulty finding affordable, stable housing. As individuals become ill, they may find themselves unable to work, while at the same time facing health care expenses that leave few resources to pay for housing. In addition, many of those persons living with AIDS struggled to afford housing even before being diagnosed with the disease. The financial vulnerability associated with AIDS, as well as the human immunodeficiency virus (HIV) that causes AIDS, results in a greater likelihood of homelessness among persons living with the disease. At the same time, those who are homeless may be more likely to engage in activities through which they could acquire or transmit HIV. Further, recent research has indicated that those individuals living with HIV who live in stable housing have better health outcomes than those who are homeless or unstably housed, and that they spend fewer days in hospitals and emergency rooms.

Congress recognized the housing needs of persons living with HIV/AIDS when it approved the Housing Opportunities for Persons with AIDS (HOPWA) program in 1990 as part of the Cranston-Gonzalez National Affordable Housing Act (P.L. 101-625). The HOPWA program, administered by the Department of Housing and Urban Development (HUD), funds short-term and permanent housing, together with supportive services, for individuals living with HIV/AIDS and their families. In addition, a small portion of funds appropriated through the Ryan White HIV/AIDS program, administered by the Department of Health and Human Services (HHS), may also be used to fund short-term housing for those living with HIV/AIDS.

In FY2012, Congress appropriated $332 million for HOPWA as part of the Consolidated Appropriations Act (P.L. 112-55). This was a reduction of $3 million from the $335 million appropriated in FY2011 and FY2010, the most funding ever appropriated for the program. Prior to FY2010, the most that had been appropriated for HOPWA was $310 million in FY2009. HOPWA funds are distributed to states and localities through both formula and competitive grants. HUD awards 90% of appropriated funds by formula to states and eligible metropolitan statistical areas (MSAs) based on population, reported cases of AIDS, and incidence of AIDS. The remaining 10% is distributed through a grant competition. Funds are used primarily for housing activities, although grant recipients must provide supportive services to those persons residing in HOPWA-funded housing.

Contents

Tables

Appendixes

Contacts

Introduction

Acquired immunodeficiency syndrome (AIDS), a disease caused by the human immunodeficiency virus (HIV), weakens the immune system, leaving individuals with the disease susceptible to infections. As of 2009, AIDS had been diagnosed and reported in an estimated 490,696 individuals living in the 50 states, the District of Columbia, and the territories.[1] These estimates do not include those diagnosed with HIV where the disease has not yet progressed to AIDS or those who have not yet been diagnosed as HIV positive but are currently living with the disease. Currently there is no cure for HIV/AIDS, and in the early years of the AIDS epidemic, those persons infected with AIDS often died quickly. In recent years, however, medications have allowed persons living with HIV and AIDS to live longer and to remain in better health.

Despite improvements in health outcomes, affordable housing remains important to many who live with HIV/AIDS. This report describes recent research that shows how housing and health status are related and the effects of stable housing on patient health. It also describes the Housing Opportunities for Persons with AIDS (HOPWA) program, the only federal program that provides housing and services specifically for persons who are HIV positive or who have AIDS, together with their families. In addition, the report describes how a small portion of funds appropriated through the Ryan White HIV/AIDS program may be used by states and local jurisdictions to provide short-term housing assistance for persons living with HIV/AIDS.

Housing Status of Persons Living with HIV/AIDS

The availability of adequate, affordable housing for persons living with HIV and AIDS has been an issue since AIDS was first identified in U.S. patients in the early 1980s. The inability to afford housing and the threat of homelessness confront many individuals living with HIV/AIDS. From the early years of the epidemic, those individuals who have been infected with HIV/AIDS face impoverishment as they become unable to work, experience high medical costs, or lose private health insurance coverage. The incidence of HIV/AIDS has also grown among low-income individuals who were economically vulnerable even before onset of the disease.[2]

Not surprisingly, researchers have found a co-occurrence between HIV/AIDS and homelessness. Homeless persons have a higher incidence of HIV/AIDS infection than the general population, while many individuals with HIV/AIDS are at risk of becoming homeless.[3] Research has found

---

[1] Note that this represents persons living with AIDS, not a cumulative total. U.S. Department of Health and Human Services, Centers for Disease Control and Prevention, *HIV Surveillance Report 2010*, vol. 22, Atlanta, GA, March 2012, pp. 56-57, table 16b, http://www.cdc.gov/hiv/surveillance/resources/reports/2010report/pdf/2010_HIV_Surveillance_Report_vol_22.pdf#Page=1.

[2] John M. Karon, Patricia L. Fleming, Richard W. Steketee, and Kevin M. DeCock, "HIV in the United States at the Turn of the Century: An Epidemic in Transition," *American Journal of Public Health* 91, no. 7 (July 2001): 1064-1065. See also, Paul Denning and Elizabeth DiNenno, *Communities in Crisis Is There a Generalized HIV Epidemic in Impoverished Urban Areas of the United States?*, Centers for Disease Control and Prevention, August 2010, http://www.cdc.gov/hiv/topics/surveillance/resources/other/pdf/poverty_poster.pdf.

[3] See, for example, D.P. Culhane, E. Gollub, R. Kuhn, and M. Shpaner, "The Co-Occurrence of AIDS and Homelessness: Results from the Integration of Administrative Databases for AIDS Surveillance and Public Shelter Utilization in Philadelphia," *Journal of Epidemiology and Community Health* 55, no. 7 (2001): 515-520. Marjorie Robertson, et al., "HIV Seroprevalence Among Homeless and Marginally Housed Adults in San Francisco," *American Journal of Public Health* 94, no. 7 (2004): 1207-1217. Angela A. Aidala and Gunjeong Lee, *Housing Services and Housing Stability Among Persons Living with HIV/AIDS*, Joseph L. Mailman School of Public Health, May 30, 2000, (continued...)

---

that rates of HIV among homeless people may be as much as three to nine times higher than among those living in stable housing.[4] Further, those who are HIV positive and homeless have been found to be more likely than those who are HIV positive and housed to engage in behaviors associated with the spread of HIV/AIDS. In one study, the use of injectable drugs, sharing needles, and exchanging sex for drugs or money were more likely among both homeless individuals and those who were unstably housed compared to those with stable housing.[5] (Those who were considered unstably housed lived in transitional housing, in jail, drug treatment or a halfway house, or were doubled up in someone else's home.)[6] When housing improved for individuals in the study, their odds of engaging in these behaviors were reduced. Another study found that homeless persons living with HIV/AIDS were almost twice as likely to engage in unprotected sex compared to those who had housing.[7] (Individuals were considered housed if they lived in a house or apartment alone or with others, a medical care facility, or a correctional institution.)[8]

Creation of the Housing Opportunities for Persons with AIDS (HOPWA) Program

In 1988, Congress established the National Commission on AIDS as part of the Health Omnibus Extension Act (P.L. 100-607) to "promote the development of a national consensus on policy concerning acquired immune deficiency syndrome (AIDS); and to study and make recommendations for a consistent national policy concerning AIDS." In April 1990, in its second interim report to the President, the commission recommended that Congress and the President provide "[f]ederal housing aid to address the multiple problems posed by HIV infection and AIDS."[9] About the same time that the commission released its report, in March of 1990, the House Committee on Banking, Finance, and Urban Affairs held a hearing about the need for housing among persons living with HIV/AIDS. Witnesses as well as committee members discussed various barriers to housing for persons living with HIV/AIDS. Among the issues confronting those persons that were discussed at the hearing were poverty, homelessness, and discrimination[10] in attempting to secure housing.[11] Another issue discussed at the hearing was the

---

(...continued)

http://www.nyhiv.org/pdfs/chain/CHAIN%20Housing%20Stability%2032.pdf.

[4] Daniel P. Kidder, Richard J. Wolitski, and Scott Royal, et al., "Access to Housing as a Structural Intervention for Homeless and Unstably Housed People Living with HIV: Rational, Methods, and Implementation of the Housing and Health Study," *AIDS and Behavior*, vol. 11, no. 6 (November 2007, supplement), pp. 149-150.

[5] Angela Aidala, Jay E. Cross, Ron Stall, David Harre, and Esther Sumartojo, "Housing Status and HIV Risk Behaviors: Implications for Prevention and Policy," *AIDS and Behavior* 9, no. 3 (2005): 251-265.

[6] Ibid., p. 254.

[7] Daniel P. Kidder, Richard J. Wolitski, and Sherri L. Pals, et al., "Housing Status and HIV Risk Behaviors Among Homeless and Housed Persons with HIV," *Journal of Acquired Immune Deficiency Syndromes*, vol. 49, no. 4 (December 1, 2008), pp. 453-454.

[8] Ibid., p. 452.

[9] The second interim report was released on April 24, 1990. Its recommendations were reprinted in National Commission on Acquired Immune Deficiency Syndrome, *Annual Report to the President and Congress*, August 1990, pp. 106-109.

[10] Individuals living with HIV/AIDS have experienced housing discrimination even though they are protected as persons with a "handicap" under the Fair Housing Act (FHA). 42 U.S.C. §§3601-3631. A number of court cases have established that the definition of "handicap" protects persons who are HIV positive and persons with AIDS. See, for example, *Baxter* v. *City of Belleville, Ill.*, 720 F.Supp. 720, 729-730 (S.D.Ill.1989), and *Support Ministries for Persons With AIDS, Inc.* v. *Village of Waterford, N.Y.*, 808 F.Supp. 120, 129-133 (N.D.N.Y. 1992).

---

eligibility for subsidized housing for persons living with the disease. A question raised during the hearing, but left unresolved, was whether persons living with HIV or AIDS met the definition of "handicap" in order to be eligible for the Section 202 Supportive Housing for the Elderly program (which also provided housing for persons with disabilities).[12] Another concern was that persons living with HIV/AIDS often had difficulty obtaining subsidized housing through mainstream HUD programs such as Public Housing and Section 8 due to the length of waiting lists; individuals often died while waiting for available units.[13]

In the 101st Congress, at least two bills were introduced that contained provisions to create a housing program specifically for persons living with AIDS. These proposed programs were called the AIDS Housing Opportunity Act (which was part of the Housing and Community Development Act of 1990, H.R. 1180) and the AIDS Opportunity Housing Act (H.R. 3423). The bills were similar, and both proposed to fund short-term and permanent housing, together with supportive services, for individuals living with AIDS and related diseases. The text from one of these bills, H.R. 1180, which included the AIDS Housing Opportunity Act, was incorporated into the Cranston-Gonzalez National Affordable Housing Act (S. 566) when it was debated and passed by the House on August 1, 1990. In conference with the Senate, the name of the housing program was changed to Housing Opportunities for Persons with AIDS (HOPWA). In addition, the several separate housing assistance programs that had been proposed in H.R. 1180—one for short-term housing, one for permanent housing supported through Section 8, and one for community residences—were consolidated into one formula grant program in which recipient communities could choose which activities to fund. The amended version of S. 566 was signed by the President on November 28, 1990, and became P.L. 101-625, the Cranston Gonzalez National Affordable Housing Act.

The HOPWA program is administered by the Department of Housing and Urban Development (HUD) and remains the only federal program solely dedicated to providing housing assistance to persons living with HIV/AIDS and their families.[14] The program addresses the need for reasonably priced housing for thousands of low-income individuals (those with incomes at or below 80% of the area median income). HOPWA was last reauthorized by the Housing and Community Development Act of 1992 (P.L. 102-550). Although authorization for HOPWA expired after FY1994, Congress continues to fund the program through annual appropriations.

(...continued)

[11] Hearing before the House Committee on Banking, Finance, and Urban Affairs, Subcommittee on Housing and Community Development, "Housing Needs of Persons with Acquired Immune Deficiency Syndrome," March 21, 1990, (hereafter Hearing on Housing Needs). See also, Statement of Representative James A. McDermott, 135 Cong. Rec. 23641, October 5, 1989.

[12] Hearing on Housing Needs, pp. 25-30. See footnote 11.

[13] U.S. Congress, House Committee on Banking, Finance, and Urban Affairs, *Housing and Community Development Act of 1990*, report to accompany H.R. 1180, 101st Cong., 2nd sess., June 21, 1990, H.Rept. 101-559.

[14] The law is codified at 42 U.S.C. §§12901-12912, with regulations at 24 C.F.R. Parts 574.3-574.655.

Distribution and Use of HOPWA Funds

Formula Grants

HOPWA program funding is distributed both by formula allocations and competitive grants. HUD awards 90% of appropriated funds by formula to states and eligible metropolitan statistical areas (MSAs) that meet the minimum AIDS case requirements according to data reported to the Centers for Disease Control and Prevention (CDC) in the previous year. (For the amounts distributed to eligible states and MSAs in recent years, see **Appendix**.) HOPWA formula funds are available through HUD's Consolidated Plan initiative. Jurisdictions applying for funds from four HUD formula grant programs, including HOPWA,[15] submit a single consolidated plan to HUD. The plan includes an assessment of community housing and development needs and a proposal that addresses those needs, using both federal funds and community resources. Communities that participate in the Consolidated Plan may receive HOPWA funds if they meet formula requirements. Formula funds are allocated in two ways:

- First, 75% of the total available formula funds, sometimes referred to by HUD as "base funding," is distributed to

  —the largest cities within metropolitan statistical areas (MSAs)[16] with populations of at least 500,000 and with 1,500 or more cumulative reported cases of AIDS (which includes those who have died); and

  —to states with at least 1,500 cases of AIDS in the areas outside of that state's eligible MSAs.[17]

- Second, 25% of total available formula funds—sometimes referred to by HUD as "bonus funding"—is distributed on the basis of AIDS incidence during the past three years.[18] Only the largest cities within MSAs that have populations of at least 500,000, with at least 1,500 reported cases of AIDS *and* that have a higher than average per capita incidence of AIDS are eligible.[19] States are not eligible for bonus funding.

Although HOPWA funds are allocated to the largest city within an MSA, these recipient cities are required to allocate funds "in a manner that addresses the needs within the metropolitan statistical area in which the city is located."[20] While the distribution of the balance of state funds is based on AIDS cases outside of eligible MSAs, states may use funds for projects in any area of the state,

---

[15] The others are the Community Development Block Grant, the Emergency Solutions Grants, and HOME.

[16] MSAs are defined as having at least one core "urbanized" area of 50,000 with the MSA comprised of "the central county or counties containing the core, plus adjacent outlying counties having a high degree of social and economic integration with the central county or counties as measured through commuting." See Office of Management and Budget, "2010 Standards for Delineating Metropolitan and Micropolitan Statistical Areas," 75 *Federal Register* 37246-37252, July 28, 2010.

[17] 42 U.S.C. §12903(c)(1)(A).

[18] AIDS incidence is measured as the number of new AIDS cases during a given time period.

[19] 42 U.S.C. §12903(c)(1)(B).

[20] 42 U.S.C. §12903(f).

---

including those that received their own funds.[21] According to HUD guidance, states should serve clients in areas outside of eligible MSAs, but the state may operate anywhere in the state because it "may be coordinating the use of all resources in a way that addresses needs more appropriately throughout the state."[22] In FY2012, 94 MSAs (including the District of Columbia) received funds, while 40 states and Puerto Rico received funds for use in the areas outside of recipient MSAs.[23] HUD jurisdictions that receive HOPWA funds may administer housing and services programs themselves or may allocate all or a portion of the funds to subgrantee private nonprofit organizations. HOPWA formula funds remain available for obligation for two years.

As a result of language included in every HUD appropriations law since FY1999 (P.L. 105-276), states do not lose formula funds if their reported AIDS cases drop below 1,500, as long as they received funding in the previous fiscal year. States generally drop below 1,500 AIDS cases when a large metropolitan area becomes separately eligible for formula funds. These states are allocated a grant on the basis of the cumulative number of AIDS cases outside of their MSAs.[24]

Competitive Grants

The remaining 10% of HOPWA funding is available through competitive grants. Funds are distributed through a national competition to two groups of grantees: (1) states and local governments that propose to provide short-term, transitional, or permanent supportive housing in areas that are not eligible for formula allocations, and (2) government agencies or nonprofit entities that propose "special projects of national significance."[25] A project of national significance is one that uses an innovative service delivery model. In determining proposals that qualify, HUD must consider the innovativeness of the proposal and its potential replicability in other communities.[26] Competitive grants may not be used to provide supportive services alone; instead, services can only be provided in conjunction with housing activities, and funds for services cannot exceed 35% of a project's budget.[27]

The competitive grants are awarded through HUD's annual SuperNOFA (Notice of Funding Availability), which is generally published in the *Federal Register* in the early spring. Since FY2000 (P.L. 106-377), Congress has required HUD to renew expiring contracts for permanent supportive housing prior to awarding funds to new projects. In FY2009 and FY2010, the amount of funds required for project renewals meant that there were no funds available for new competitive grants.[28] In FY2011, HUD awarded approximately $9 million in new competitive

---

[21] 24 C.F.R. §574.3.

[22] U.S. Department of Housing and Urban Development, *2011 HOPWA Formula Operating Instructions*, April 28, 2011, p. 3, http://www.hudhre.info/documents/2011Operating_Formula.pdf.

[23] U.S. Department of Housing and Urban Development, Office of Community Planning and Development, Formula Allocations for FY2012, http://www.hud.gov/offices/cpd/about/budget/budget12/.

[24] According to HUD, the states that have retained funding under this provision are Arizona, Connecticut, Delaware, Hawaii, Massachusetts, Minnesota, Nevada, New Mexico, Oklahoma, and Utah. See U.S. Department of Housing and Urban Development, *Congressional Justifications for FY2011*, p. Z-12, http://hud.gov/offices/cfo/reports/2011/cjs/hofpwAIDS2011.pdf.

[25] 42 U.S.C. §12903(c)(3).

[26] Ibid.

[27] See, for example, U.S. Department of Housing and Urban Development, "FY2008 Notice of Funding Availability Housing Opportunities for Persons with AIDS," 73 *Federal Register* 27266, May 12, 2008.

[28] See U.S. Department of Housing and Urban Development, *Congressional Justifications for 2012 Estimates*, p. Z-13, (continued...)

---

grants to seven projects.[29] HUD anticipates that it will not fund any new grants again in FY2012.[30] Beginning in FY2006, competitive funds remain available for obligation for three years (from FY2002 through FY2005, competitive funds had been available only for two years). The extension makes the rules for HOPWA's competitive program consistent with those of other competitive programs advertised in HUD's SuperNOFA.

Eligibility for HOPWA-Funded Housing

In the HOPWA program, individuals are eligible for housing if they are either HIV positive or if they are diagnosed with AIDS.[31] In general, clients must also be low income, meaning that their income does not exceed 80% of the area median income.[32] HUD reports area median incomes for metropolitan areas and non-metropolitan counties on an annual basis.[33] Housing and some supportive services are available for family members of persons living with AIDS. When a person living in HOPWA-supported housing dies, his or her family members are given a grace period during which they may remain in the housing.[34] This period may not exceed one year, however.

Individuals who are HIV positive or living with AIDS may also be eligible for other HUD-assisted housing for persons with disabilities. However, infection itself may not be sufficient to meet the definition of disability in these other programs. For example, in the case of housing developed prior to the mid-1990s under the Section 202 Supportive Housing for the Elderly program and those units developed under the Section 811 Supportive Housing for Persons with Disabilities program, an individual who is HIV positive or has AIDS must also meet the statutory definition of disability (in which HIV/AIDS status alone is not sufficient) to be eligible for housing.[35] The project-based Section 8 and Public Housing programs may also set aside units or entire developments for persons with disabilities. The definition of disability for these programs does "not exclude persons who have the disease of acquired immunodeficiency syndrome or any

---

(...continued)

http://portal hud.gov/hudportal/documents/huddoc?id=HOPWA_2012.pdf.

[29] U.S. Department of Housing and Urban Development, "HUD Awards $8.8 Million to Improve Housing and Services for Families and Individuals Living with AIDS," press release, September 21, 2011, http://portal.hud.gov/hudportal/HUD?src=/press/press_releases_media_advisories/2011/HUDNo.11-225.

[30] *FY2012 Budget Justifications*, p. Z-13.

[31] The HOPWA statute defines an eligible person as one "with acquired immunodeficiency syndrome or a related disease." 42 U.S.C. §12902(12). The regulations have further specified that "acquired immunodeficiency syndrome or related diseases means the disease of acquired immunodeficiency syndrome or any conditions arising from the etiologic agent for acquired immunodeficiency syndrome, including infection with the human immunodeficiency virus (HIV)." 24 C.F.R. §574.3.

[32] 42 U.S.C. §12908 and §12909. The statutory provisions regarding short-term housing and community residences do not require individuals to be low income, although to be eligible for short-term housing a person must be homeless or at risk of homelessness. See 42 U.S.C. §12907 and §12910.

[33] U.S. Department of Housing and Urban Development, Office of Policy Development and Research, *Fiscal Year 2010 HUD Income Limits Briefing Material*, May 13, 2010, p. 1, http://www.huduser.org/portal/datasets/il/il10/IncomeLimitsBriefingMaterial_FY10.pdf. Tables showing area median incomes in recent years are available at http://www.huduser.org/datasets/il.html.

[34] 24 C.F.R. §574.310(e).

[35] For more information about housing for persons with disabilities and the definitions of disability under these programs, see CRS Report RL34728, *Section 811 and Other HUD Housing Programs for Persons with Disabilities*, by Libby Perl.

---

conditions arising from the etiologic agent" for AIDS.[36] However, the definition does not indicate whether the status of being HIV positive or having AIDS is alone sufficient to be considered disabled.

Eligible Uses of HOPWA Funds

HOPWA grantees may use funds for a wide range of housing, social services, program planning, and development costs. Supportive services must be provided together with housing. Formula grantees may also choose to provide supportive services not in conjunction with housing, although the focus of the HOPWA program is housing activities. Allowable activities include the following:

- *The Development and Operation of Multi-Unit Community Residences, Including the Provision of Supportive Services for Persons Who Live in the Residences.*[37] Funds may be used for the construction, rehabilitation, and acquisition of facilities, for payment of operating costs, and for technical assistance in developing the community residence.

- *Short-Term Rental, Mortgage, and Utility Assistance to Persons Living with AIDS Who Are Homeless or at Risk of Homelessness.*[38] Funds may be used to acquire and/or rehabilitate facilities that will be used to provide short-term housing, as well as to make payments on behalf of tenants or homeowners, and to provide supportive services. Funds may not be used to construct short-term housing facilities.[39] Residents may not stay in short-term housing facilities more than 60 days in any 6-month period, and may not receive short-term rental, mortgage, and utility assistance for more than 21 weeks in any 52-week period. These limits are subject to waiver by HUD, however, if a project sponsor is making an attempt to provide permanent supportive housing for residents and has been unable to do so. Funds may also be used to pay operating and administrative expenses.

- *Project-Based or Tenant-Based Rental Assistance for Permanent Supportive Housing, Including Shared Housing Arrangements.*[40] In general, tenants must pay approximately 30% of their income toward rent.[41] Grant recipients must ensure that residents receive supportive services, and funds may also be used for administrative costs in providing rental assistance.

- *The New Construction or Acquisition and Rehabilitation of Property for Single-Room Occupancy Dwellings.*[42]

---

[36] 42 U.S.C. §1437a(b)(3).

[37] 42 U.S.C. §12910.

[38] 42 U.S.C. §12907.

[39] HOWPA funds may only be used for construction of community residences and single-room occupancy dwellings. See 24 C.F.R. §574.300(b)(4).

[40] 42 U.S.C. §12908.

[41] See 24 C.F.R. §574.310(d).

[42] 42 U.S.C. §12909.

- *Supportive Services, Which Include Health Assessments, Counseling for Those with Addictions to Drugs and Alcohol, Nutritional Assistance, Assistance with Daily Living, Day Care, and Assistance in Applying for Other Government Benefits.*[43]

- *Housing Information Such as Counseling and Referral Services.*[44] Assistance may include fair housing counseling for those experiencing discrimination.[45]

The majority of HOPWA funds are used to provide housing. According to HUD, for the 2010-2011 program year, 66% of HOPWA funding was used for housing assistance such as rent and building operating costs.[46] An additional 4% was used to help individuals find housing, 2% for housing development, and 20% was used for supportive services. Of the amounts used for housing activities, 76% was used to support tenants in permanent housing, of whom more than 95% remained stably housed during the year.[47] Grantee performance reports indicate that clients who receive housing assistance through HOPWA are often at the lowest income levels; in its FY2013 Congressional Budget Justifications, HUD estimated that 75% of households served have extremely low incomes (at or below 30% of area median income) and 16% have very low incomes (at or below 50% of area median income).[48]

HOPWA Program Formula and Funding

The HOPWA Formula

The HOPWA method for allocating formula funds has been an ongoing issue because the cumulative number of AIDS cases—including those who have died—is used to distribute funds rather than the current number of people living with AIDS, and, potentially, HIV. In 1997, GAO released a report regarding the performance of the HOPWA program in which it recommended that HUD look at recent changes to the formula used by the Ryan White CARE Act (now called the Ryan White HIV/AIDS program) to "determine what legislative revisions are needed to make the HOPWA formula more reflective of current AIDS cases."[49] (At the time of the GAO report, Congress had recently changed the CARE Act formula to use estimates of persons living with AIDS instead of cumulative AIDS cases.)[50] In response to the GAO report, the House Appropriations Committee included the GAO language in its report accompanying the FY1998

---

[43] 24 C.F.R. §574.300(b)(7).

[44] 42 U.S.C. §12906.

[45] 24 C.F.R. §574.300(b)(1).

[46] U.S. Department of Housing and Urban Development, *HOPWA National Performance Profile 2010-2011 Program Year*, http://www.hudhre.info/hopwa_Reports/NP_Combined_PY10_11.pdf.

[47] Ibid. The percent stably housed includes those living in permanent dedicated housing units as well as those receiving tenant-based rental assistance.

[48] U.S. Department of Housing and Urban Development, *Congressional Justifications for 2013 Estimates*, p. U-14, http://portal hud.gov/hudportal/documents/huddoc?id=Housing_AIDS.pdf.

[49] U.S. Government Accountability Office, *HUD's Program for Persons with AIDS*, GAO/RCED-97-62, March 1997, p. 27, http://www.gao.gov/archive/1997/rc97062.pdf.

[50] Ryan White CARE Act Amendments of 1996, P.L. 104-146. In 2006, when the Ryan White HIV/AIDS program was reauthorized as part of the Ryan White HIV/AIDS Treatment Modernization Act of 2006 (P.L. 109-415), the formula began to incorporate living HIV cases in addition to living AIDS cases.

HUD Appropriations Act (P.L. 105-65) and directed HUD to make recommendations to Congress about its findings regarding an update to the formula.[51]

In response to the FY1998 Appropriations Act, HUD issued a report to Congress in 1999 that proposed changes that could be made to the HOPWA formula.[52] The proposed formula in HUD's 1999 report would have used an estimate of persons living with AIDS (instead of all cumulative AIDS cases), together with housing costs, to distribute formula funds. It also would have included a protection for existing grantees. Those recommendations were not adopted by Congress.

A 2006 Government Accountability Office (GAO) report again looked at the way in which the HOPWA formula allocates funds. The report found that use of the cumulative number of AIDS cases resulted in disproportionate funding per living AIDS case depending on the jurisdiction. The GAO report looked at FY2004 HOPWA allocations and found that the amount of money grantees received per living AIDS case ranged from $387 per person to $1,290.[53] According to the report, if only living AIDS cases had been counted in that year, 92 of 117 grantees would have received more formula funding, while 25 would have received less.[54]

While no legislation to change the HOPWA formula has been introduced since the 109th Congress,[55] nearly every Administration budget since FY2007 has discussed the need to change the formula. In each of President Bush's budgets from FY2007 through FY2009, the Administration proposed to change the way in which HOPWA funds are distributed. The FY2009 budget stated that "[w]hereas the current formula distributes formula grant resources by the cumulative number of AIDS cases, the revised formula will account for the present number of people living with AIDS, as well as differences in housing costs in the qualifying areas." The President's FY2007 and FY2008 budgets contained nearly identical language. HUD's budget justifications for FY2009 elaborated somewhat on the Administration's proposal to change the HOPWA distribution formula. HUD's explanation indicated that a new formula would use the number of persons living with AIDS, and that eventually, when consistent data on the number of persons living with HIV become available, that measure might also be used in determining the distribution of HOPWA funding.[56]

As part of President Obama's FY2010 budget, the HUD budget justifications stated that HUD would review the formula and "make related recommendations at a future time."[57] The Administration's *National HIV/AIDS Strategy*, released in July 2010, stated that HUD would work with Congress to "develop a plan (including seeking statutory changes if necessary) to shift

[51] See U.S. Congress, House Committee on Appropriations, Subcommittee on VA, HUD, and Independent Agencies, *Departments of Veterans Affairs and Housing and Urban Development and Independent Agencies Appropriations Bill*, report to accompany H.R. 2158, 105th Cong., 1st sess., July 11, 1997, H.Rept. 105-175, pp. 33-34.

[52] U.S. Department of Housing and Urban Development, *1999 Report on the Performance of the Housing Opportunities for Persons with AIDS Program*, October 6, 1999.

[53] U.S. Government Accountability Office, *Changes Needed to Improve the Distribution of Ryan White CARE Act and Housing Funds*, GAO-06-332, February 2006, p. 23, http://www.gao.gov/new.items/d06332.pdf.

[54] Ibid., p. 24.

[55] Two bills in the 109th Congress (S. 2339 and H.R. 5009) would have changed the way that HOPWA formula funds are allocated by counting the number of "reported living cases of HIV disease" instead of cumulative AIDS cases. Neither bill was enacted.

[56] U.S. Department of Housing and Urban Development, *Congressional Justifications for FY2009*, p. Q-2, http://www.hud.gov/offices/cfo/reports/2009/cjs/cpd1.pdf.

[57] *FY2010 Congressional Budget Justifications*, p. X-13.

to HIV/AIDS case reporting as a basis for formula grants for HOPWA funding."[58] The FY2012 and FY2013 HUD Congressional Budget Justification for HOPWA echoed this goal. Since the release of the *National HIV/AIDS Strategy*, HUD has solicited comments from interested policy advocates, grantees, and HOPWA clients about whether and how the formula might be changed.

HOPWA Funding

As a result of advances in medical science and in the care and treatment of persons living with HIV and AIDS, individuals are living longer with the disease.[59] As the number of those with AIDS grows, so do the jurisdictions that qualify for formula-based HOPWA funds. Since 1999, there has been a steady increase in the number of jurisdictions that meet the eligibility test to receive formula-based HOPWA funds. Funding for the HOPWA program has increased in almost every year since the program was created, with the exception of FY2005 through FY2007, when funding dropped from the FY2004 level of $295 million. (See **Table 1**.) In FY2010 and FY2011, the appropriation was the highest ever for the program—$335 million in each year, though the FY2011 appropriations law (P.L. 112-10) imposed an across-the-board rescission of 0.2% on all discretionary accounts, reducing the total for HOPWA to about $334.3 million. The FY2012 HOPWA appropriation was $332 million (P.L. 112-55). For information about proposed funding in FY2013, see CRS Report R42517, *Department of Housing and Urban Development (HUD): FY2013 Appropriations*, coordinated by Maggie McCarty.

The number of households receiving HOPWA housing assistance (including short-term housing assistance, housing provided through community residences, or rental assistance in permanent housing) has generally declined from FY2003 through FY2011. (See **Table 1**.) Between FY2003 and FY2009, the number of households served dropped from 78,467 to 58,367.[60] With increased funding, however, the total households served went up in FY2010 to 60,669 and then fell slightly in FY2011 to 60,234. These general reductions in households served could be due to a number of factors, including the growth in jurisdictions eligible for HOPWA grants (which have increased from 111 in FY2003 to 135 in FY2012), the amount of available funds, and housing costs.

---

[58] *National HIV/AIDS Strategy Federal Implementation Plan*, July 2010, p. 28, http://aids.gov/federal-resources/policies/national-hiv-aids-strategy/nhas-implementation.pdf.

[59] For example, researchers who analyzed data from 25 states found that from 1996 to 2005, average life expectancy after HIV diagnosis increased from 10.5 to 22 5 years. See Kathleen McDavid Harrison, Ruiguang Song, and Xinjian Zhang, "Life Expectancy after HIV Diagnosis Based on National HIV Surveillance Data from 25 States, United States," *Journal of Acquired Immune Deficiency Syndromes*, vol. 53, no. 1 (January 2010), pp. 124-130.

[60] HUD provides estimates of the numbers of households served in its annual Performance and Accountability Reports. The most recent is the *FY2009 Performance and Accountability Report*, November 16, 2009, p. 349, http://www.hud.gov/offices/cfo/reports/hudfy2009par.pdf.

**Table 1. HOPWA Funding and Eligible Jurisdictions,
FY2001-FY2012 and FY2013 Proposal**

Fiscal Year	Number of Qualifying Jurisdictions	Households Receiving Housing Assistance[a]	President's Request (dollars in thousands)	Appropriations (dollars in thousands)[b]
2001	105	72,117	260,000	257,432
2002	108	74,964	277,432	277,432
2003	111	78,467	292,000	290,102
2004	117	70,779	297,000	294,751
2005	121	67,012	294,800	281,728
2006	122	67,000	268,000	286,110
2007	123	67,850	300,100	286,110
2008	127	62,210	300,100	300,100
2009	131	58,367	300,100	310,000
2010	133	60,669	310,000	335,000
2011	134	60,234	340,000	334,330[c]
2012	135	—	335,000	332,000
2013	—	—	330,000	—

Source: Table prepared by the Congressional Research Service based on data from the Department of Housing and Urban Development budget justifications and P.L. 112-55 (number of qualifying jurisdictions and appropriation levels), FY2001 through FY2012 President's Budget Appendices (President's request), the FY2004, FY2006, FY2007, FY2008, and FY2009 HUD Performance and Accountability Reports (number of households assisted through FY2009), and the FY2012-FY2013 budget justifications (households assisted for FY2010 and FY2011). For a breakdown of formula funding by jurisdiction, see the **Appendix**.

a. Housing assistance includes short-term assistance with rent, mortgage, or utilities; residence in short-term housing facilities; housing provided through community residences and single-room occupancy dwel ings; and rental assistance for permanent supportive housing.

b. Includes rescissions.

c. The FY2011 Department of Defense and Full-Year Appropriation Act (P.L. 112-10) contained an across-the-board rescission of 0.2% for all discretionary accounts. The rescission reduced the HOPWA appropriation from $335 million to approximately $334.3 million.

Housing Funded Through the Ryan White HIV/AIDS Program

In addition to funds for housing provided through HUD, funds appropriated to the Department of Health and Human Services (HHS) Ryan White HIV/AIDS program may be used to provide short-term housing assistance to persons living with HIV/AIDS. The Ryan White Comprehensive AIDS Resources Emergency Act (P.L. 101-381) established the Ryan White program in 1990. The program provides funds to states and metropolitan areas to help pay for health care and supportive services for persons living with HIV/AIDS (referred to as "support services" in the statute).[61] The statute governing the use of Ryan White funds does not specifically list housing as an eligible activity for which grantees may use funds. However, the statute provides that grantees may use Ryan White funds to provide support services for persons living with HIV and AIDS. These services are defined as those "that are needed for individuals with HIV/AIDS to achieve their medical outcomes."[62] In 1999, the HIV/AIDS Bureau of the Health Resources and Services Administration (HRSA) within HHS released policy guidance regarding the type of housing that Ryan White grantees could provide for their clients (Policy Notice 99-02).[63] According to the guidance, grantees may use funds for housing referral services and for emergency or short-term housing. Ryan White funds must be the payer of last resort, meaning that other sources of funds for housing must be exhausted before using Ryan White funds. In 2008, nearly 33,000 persons living with an HIV positive diagnosis received some sort of housing service through the Ryan White HIV/AIDS program.[64]

Initially, the policy regarding use of Ryan White funds for housing did not require that specific time limits be placed on short-term housing. In its report regarding the guidance, HRSA stated: "Although we are restricting the policy to transitional/temporary housing, we don't define 'transitional/temporary.' Because we don't know yet what the recent changes in medical treatment of HIV/AIDS mean to the evolution of the epidemic, it is foolish to adopt any definition of 'short-term.'"[65] However, when the Ryan White program was reauthorized in 2006, the new law limited the amount of grants to states and urban areas that could be used for supportive services to no more than 25% by requiring that at least 75% of funds be used for "core medical services."[66] Previously the law did not limit the amount of funds that could be used for support services.

In December 2006, in response to the "more restrictive funding limits established for support services in the 2006 reauthorization," HHS issued a proposed policy notice to limit the amount of time that any client could spend in Ryan White-funded transitional housing to 24 months in a lifetime, effective retroactively.[67] This would have meant that those individuals who had already exhausted the 24-month time period would not be able to receive housing benefits. After receiving over 200 comments regarding the policy proposal, HHS eventually removed the provision requiring retroactive application of the 24-month lifetime limit and released a final

---

[61] For more information about the Ryan White program, see CRS Report RL33279, *The Ryan White HIV/AIDS Program*, by Judith A. Johnson.

[62] 42 U.S.C. §300ff-14(d)(1) and §300ff-22(c)(1). At the time that HHS established its housing policy, the statute stated that funds could be used "for the purpose of delivering or enhancing HIV-related outpatient and ambulatory health and support services, including case management and comprehensive treatment services ... " The statute was amended to read as stated in the text of this report as part of the Ryan White HIV/AIDS Treatment Modernization Act of 2006, P.L. 109-415.

[63] Policy Notice 99-02 is reproduced in U.S. Department of Health and Human Services, Health Resources and Services Administration, *Housing is Health Care A Guide to Implementing the HIV/AIDS Bureau (HAB) Ryan White CARE Act Housing Policy*, 2001, p. 3, ftp://ftp.hrsa.gov/hab/housingmanualjune.pdf (hereinafter, *Housing is Health Care*).

[64] U.S. Department of Health and Human Services, Health Resources and Services Administration, HIV/AIDS Bureau, *Going the Distance 20 Years of Leadership, A Legacy of Care 2010 Ryan White HIV/AIDS Progress Report*, August 2010, p. 48, http://hab.hrsa.gov/data/files/2010progressrpt.pdf.

[65] *Housing is Health Care*, p. 7. See footnote 63.

[66] The program was reauthorized in the Ryan White HIV/AIDS Treatment Modernization Act of 2006 (P.L. 109-415). See Section 105.

[67] U.S. Department of Health and Human Services, "HIV/AIDS Bureau Policy Notice 99-02," 71 *Federal Register* 70781, December 6, 2006.

---

policy notice on February 27, 2008 (Amendment #1 to Policy Notice 99-02).[68] The policy took effect on March 27, 2008. However, as the 24-month deadline approached, in February 2010 HRSA released another notice announcing that it was rescinding Amendment #1 to Policy Notice 99-02, and that grantees would not be required to enforce the previous 24-month limit on housing services.[69] HRSA also noted that it would be "undertaking a comprehensive review of the Housing Policy."[70]

On May 12, 2011, HRSA released a final notice (Notice 11-01) laying out how Ryan White funds may be used for housing.[71] Ryan White Parts A, B, and D funding (grants to urban areas, states, and public or nonprofit entities) can be used to fund housing search assistance and "short-term or emergency housing." Although Notice 11-01 did not specifically limit the amount of time that housing can be funded, it defined "short-term or emergency housing" as:

> transitional in nature and for the purposes of moving or maintaining an individual or family in a long-term, stable living situation. Thus, such assistance cannot be permanent and must be accompanied by a strategy to identify, relocate, and/or ensure the individual or family is moved to, or capable of maintaining, a long-term, stable living situation.[72]

In addition, the notice strongly encouraged grantees or local planning bodies to define short-term housing themselves, recommending that they consider adopting the HUD definition of transitional housing: 24 months.[73]

Under Notice 11-01, housing must either provide medical or supportive services, or, if it does not provide these services, the housing must be necessary for clients to gain access to or compliance with medical care. Ryan White funds may not be used to make direct payments to clients or for mortgage payments, and Ryan White must be the payer of last resort.

---

[68] U.S. Department of Health and Human Services, "HIV/AIDS Bureau Policy Notice 99-02 Amendment #1," 73 *Federal Register* 10260-10261, February 26, 2008.

[69] U.S. Department of Health and Human Services, Health Resources and Services Administration, "HIV/AIDS Bureau: Policy Notice 99-02 Amendment #1," 75 *Federal Register* 6672-6673, February 10, 2010.

[70] Ibid.

[71] U.S. Department of Health and Human Services, Health Resources and Services Administration, "HIV/AIDS Bureau Policy Notice 11–01 (Replaces Policy Notice 99–02)," 76 *Federal Register* 27649-27651, May 12, 2011.

[72] Ibid., p. 27650.

[73] Transitional housing is defined in the law governing the HUD Homeless Assistance Grants as "housing the purpose of which is to facilitate the movement of individuals and families experiencing homelessness to permanent housing within 24 months or such longer period as the Secretary determines necessary." 42 U.S.C. §11360(29).

The Relationship Between Stable Housing and Health Outcomes

As mentioned earlier in this report, HIV/AIDS status is associated with homelessness: those persons who are homeless are more likely to be HIV positive than those who are housed. In addition, recent research has found that the health outcomes of homeless individuals living with HIV/AIDS may be improved with stable housing. In response to evidence from recent studies, the Administration's *National HIV/AIDS Strategy*, published in 2010, acknowledged that "access to housing is an important precursor to getting many people into a stable treatment regimen. Individuals living with HIV who lack stable housing are more likely to delay HIV care, have poorer access to regular care, are less likely to receive optimal antiretroviral therapy, and are less likely to adhere to therapy."[74] The *National HIV/AIDS Strategy* included pursuing the goal of housing as one of the ways to increase access to care and improve health outcomes for individuals living with HIV and AIDS.[75]

This section of the report gives a short overview of several studies that have examined how access to stable housing influences health outcomes for those living with HIV and AIDS.

Community Health Advisory & Information Network (CHAIN) Project Data

The CHAIN Project is a longitudinal study, begun in 1994, of a sample of individuals who are living with HIV/AIDS in New York City and the northern suburbs. In 2007, researchers released a study that used the CHAIN data to examine the effects of stable housing on health care for individuals living with HIV and AIDS.[76]

The study looked at those who were unstably housed—meaning that they were either living in some form of transitional housing; in a jail, drug treatment facility, or halfway house; in a hospice; or temporarily living in someone else's home—or who were homeless, meaning that they were living in a shelter or place not meant for human habitation. Researchers measured the likelihood of six scenarios involving the receipt or continuity of both medical care in general and appropriate HIV medical care. In general, individuals who were unstably housed were less likely to enter into and retain both medical care and appropriate HIV care.[77] However, the likelihood of obtaining and retaining medical care increased if individuals received some form of housing assistance.[78] In addition, receipt of mental health services and social services case management had a statistically significant relationship to individuals entering into and retaining medical care.

---

[74] *National HIV/AIDS Strategy for the United States*, July 13, 2010, p. 28, http://www.whitehouse.gov/sites/default/files/uploads/NHAS.pdf.

[75] Ibid., pp. 27-28.

[76] Angela A. Aidala, Gunjeong Lee, and David M. Abramson, et al., "Housing Need, Housing Assistance, and Connection to HIV Medical Care," *Aids and Behavior*, vol. 11, no. 6 (November 2007, supplement), pp. S101-S115.

[77] The statistical significance of the likelihood varied among the models used. See Table 3, pp. S110-S111 for significance.

[78] Findings were statistically significant in all but one of six models—continuity of appropriate HIV medical care.

Housing and Health Study

In the Housing and Health Study, HUD, together with the CDC, provided HIV positive individuals who were homeless or at severe risk of homelessness with HOPWA-funded rental housing. (The study considered individuals to be at severe risk of homelessness if they frequently moved from one temporary housing situation to another.) Those individuals in the comparison group received services, including assistance with finding housing, but did not receive HOPWA-funded housing.[79] Despite the differences in rental assistance provided between the treatment and comparison groups, both groups had a statistically significant increase in stable housing.[80] After 18 months, 82% of HOPWA-assisted renters and 52% of individuals in the comparison group were living in their own housing. Perhaps due to the fact that the comparison group also had some success in achieving and maintaining housing, both groups saw statistically significant improvements in health outcomes. After 18 months, both groups had fewer emergency room visits, fewer hospitalizations, reduced opportunistic infections (those infections that occur due to weakened immune systems), and reduced use of medical care generally. Self-reported depression and perceived stress saw improvement as well.

Chicago Housing for Health Partnership Study

The Chicago Housing for Health Partnership study identified homeless individuals with chronic illnesses, including HIV, for participation. Among those who participated in the study, 36% were HIV positive. The treatment group received housing funded through either HOPWA or HUD's Supportive Housing Program for homeless individuals, while the comparison, or usual care group, received available supportive services but no separate assistance with rent. The study found that, after 12 months, the group receiving housing assistance had higher rates of intact immunity compared to the comparison group and were more likely to have undetectable viral loads.[81] There was no statistically significant difference between CD4 counts for the treatment and usual care group. (Very generally, CD4 counts are a measure of immune system strength.) At the conclusion of the study, the treatment group was found to have spent fewer days in emergency rooms and hospitals during the 18 month period in which the researchers followed participants. Specifically, compared to those in the usual care group, those in the treatment group showed 29% reduction in hospitalizations, a 29% reduction in the number of days spent in the hospital, and a 24% reduction in visits to the emergency room.[82]

---

[79] The methodology of the study is described in Daniel P. Kidder, Richard J. Wolitski, and Scott Royal, et al., "Access to Housing as a Structural Intervention for Homeless and Unstably Housing People Living with HIV: Rationale, Methods, and Implementation of the Housing and Health Study," *AIDS and Behavior*, vol. 11, no. 6 (November 2007, supplement), pp. 149-161.

[80] Richard J. Wolitski, Daniel P. Kidder, and Sherri L. Pals, et al., "Randomized Trial of the Effects of Housing Assistance on the Health and Risk Behaviors of Homeless and Unstably Housing People Living with HIV," *AIDS & Behavior*, vol. 14, no. 3 (2010), pp. 493-503.

[81] David Buchanan, Romina Kee, and Laura S. Sadowski, et al., "The Health Impact of Supportive Housing for HIV-Positive Homeless Patients: A Randomized Controlled Trial," *American Journal of Public Health*, vol. 99, no. S3 (November 2009), pp. S675-S680.

[82] Laura S. Sadowski, Romina A. Kee, and Tyler J. VanderWeele, et al., "Effects of a Housing and Case Management Program on Emergency Department Visits and Hospitalizations Among Chronically Ill Homeless Adults," *Journal of the American Medical Association*, vol. 301, no. 17 (May 6, 2009), pp. 1775-1776.

Appendix. Recent HOPWA Formula Allocations

Table A-1. HOPWA Formula Allocations, FY2004-FY2012

MSA, State, or Territory	FY2004	FY2005	FY2006	FY2007	FY2008	FY2009	FY2010	FY2011	FY2012
Alabama State Program	1,139,000	1,117,000	1,145,000	1,163,000	1,241,000	1,299,792	1,403,821	1,402,039	1,419,006
Birmingham	520,000	497,000	511,000	516,000	538,000	554,848	593,523	586,116	582,166
Arkansas State Program	752,000	723,000	707,000	720,000	766,000	797,682	531,915	544,150	543,382
Little Rock	—	—	—	—	—	—	317,437	319,590	320,567
Arizona State Program	164,000	164,000	173,000	180,000	191,000	198,919	219,282	223,148	230,334
Phoenix	1,434,000	1,391,000	1,433,000	1,456,000	1,541,000	1,608,397	1,769,291	1,779,736	1,808,832
Tucson	402,000	390,000	389,000	390,000	411,000	420,497	453,391	453,761	459,084
California State Program	3,042,000	2,869,000	2,929,000	2,926,000	2,746,000	2,557,875	2,746,244	2,694,723	2,696,922
Bakersfield[a]	—	—	—	—	323,000	472,334	635,917	375,881	384,879
Fresno[a]	—	—	—	—	—	315,824	346,048	352,275	358,363
Los Angeles	10,476,000	11,848,000	10,310,000	10,393,000	10,437,000	10,764,091	12,384,800	12,627,562	15,305,260
Oakland	2,006,000	1,879,000	1,905,000	1,896,000	1,952,000	2,038,921	2,208,481	2,514,177	2,673,899
Riverside	1,772,000	1,683,000	1,684,000	1,689,000	1,751,000	1,850,429	1,990,870	1,970,602	1,981,582
Sacramento	844,000	795,000	786,000	784,000	818,000	844,003	906,991	884,723	900,755
San Diego	2,683,000	2,527,000	2,549,000	2,551,000	2,646,000	2,731,528	2,935,661	2,884,983	2,883,128
San Francisco	8,562,000	8,466,000	8,070,000	8,189,000	8,193,000	9,233,417	9,977,748	9,782,816	9,731,577
San Jose	792,000	736,000	738,000	739,000	767,000	796,679	871,489	861,520	878,197
Santa Anna	1,436,000	1,342,000	1,359,000	1,345,000	1,402,000	1,458,807	1,568,178	1,540,447	1,548,618
Colorado State Program	366,000	354,000	364,000	363,000	379,000	392,424	425,407	424,707	426,632

MSA, State, or Territory	FY2004	FY2005	FY2006	FY2007	FY2008	FY2009	FY2010	FY2011	FY2012
Denver	1,424,000	1,342,000	1,359,000	1,361,000	1,414,000	1,452,390	1,572,773	1,565,263	1,573,947
Connecticut State Program	251,000	242,000	253,000	252,000	263,000	268,902	286,319	283,878	282,574
Bridgeport	779,000	717,000	737,000	739,000	771,000	854,931	846,219	832,063	829,320
Hartford	1,023,000	1,285,000	1,108,000	1,098,000	1,140,000	1,084,029	1,153,422	1,131,275	1,126,735
New Haven	1,232,000	1,624,000	1,178,000	1,075,000	946,000	963,113	1,021,853	1,001,946	989,999
Washington, DC	11,802,000	10,535,000	11,370,000	11,118,000	11,541,000	12,213,518	14,118,841	13,795,546	13,623,582
Delaware State Program	164,000	162,000	166,000	167,000	179,000	186,286	202,783	205,796	204,213
Wilmington[b]	798,000	703,000	679,000	552,000	604,000	651,902	771,469	686,951	639,156
Florida State Program	4,063,000	3,581,000	3,312,000	3,316,000	3,191,000	3,012,662	3,655,741	3,680,729	3,714,625
Cape Coral[c]	—	—	336,000	332,000	350,000	368,963	402,434	451,881	411,395
Deltona[d]	—	—	—	—	—	312,215	—	—	—
Fort Lauderdale	6,240,000	6,106,000	6,637,000	6,878,000	7,351,000	7,545,922	8,646,967	9,305,740	9,482,644
Jacksonville	1,564,000	1,624,000	1,587,000	1,630,000	1,988,000	2,265,720	2,510,630	2,815,995	2,584,823
Lakeland[c]	—	378,000	445,000	418,000	509,000	491,383	545,040	635,095	678,078
Miami	10,715,000	10,351,000	11,189,000	11,689,000	12,370,000	12,599,526	12,935,584	12,498,939	12,163,466
Orlando	3,189,000	2,871,000	2,906,000	2,895,000	3,234,000	3,533,132	3,347,552	3,640,338	3,401,180
Palm Bay[c]	—	—	—	—	311,000	317,829	341,871	340,775	340,949
Sarasota/Bradenton[c]	397,000	548,000	390,000	391,000	409,000	421,099	460,283	459,410	457,699
Tampa	2,389,000	3,049,000	2,542,000	2,772,000	3,193,000	3,449,810	3,721,763	3,548,685	3,190,576
West Palm Beach	3,836,000	3,426,000	3,595,000	3,235,000	3,271,000	3,200,060	3,466,709	3,478,287	3,404,924
Georgia State Program	1,515,000	1,527,000	1,576,000	1,621,000	1,744,000	1,860,455	2,025,746	2,019,428	2,038,769
Atlanta	4,899,000	6,592,000	5,290,000	6,801,000	7,034,000	8,788,464	9,224,086	10,142,432	8,539,053
Augusta	373,000	418,000	376,000	394,000	385,000	398,640	429,792	425,918	425,840
Hawaii State Program	181,000	169,000	162,000	160,000	164,000	168,039	181,691	178,357	176,906

MSA, State, or Territory	FY2004	FY2005	FY2006	FY2007	FY2008	FY2009	FY2010	FY2011	FY2012
Honolulu	452,000	428,000	429,000	419,000	433,000	444,761	473,440	472,726	477,883
Iowa State Program	347,000	329,000	330,000	336,000	354,000	367,359	400,137	405,944	409,416
Illinois State Program	864,000	827,000	875,000	875,000	916,000	945,467	1,014,962	1,015,666	1,028,784
Chicago	8,338,000	5,379,000	5,561,000	5,572,000	5,819,000	5,993,040	6,426,836	6,371,215	6,417,879
Indiana State Program	836,000	806,000	818,000	822,000	863,000	892,730	971,314	980,761	980,105
Indianapolis	759,000	738,000	751,000	752,000	782,000	806,705	878,589	884,925	895,610
Kansas State Program	363,000	349,000	331,000	332,000	346,000	357,333	384,683	384,759	386,858
Kentucky State Program	423,000	407,000	410,000	408,000	431,000	452,782	493,906	501,578	510,929
Louisville	462,000	443,000	447,000	453,000	476,000	502,511	554,887	553,834	557,629
Louisiana State Program	940,000	932,000	951,000	975,000	1,034,000	1,090,045	1,203,335	1,234,375	1,266,439
Baton Rouge	1,813,000	1,659,000	1,572,000	1,409,000	1,433,000	1,797,197	2,225,972	2,303,702	2,552,872
New Orleans	2,992,000	3,398,000	2,997,000	2,914,000	2,769,000	3,089,672	3,385,486	3,416,072	3,584,653
Massachusetts State Program	525,000	178,000	168,000	166,000	173,000	180,471	194,639	197,121	1,878,288
Boston	1,829,000	1,721,000	1,719,000	1,690,000	1,747,000	1,779,243	1,889,165	1,884,046	197,288
Lowell	659,000	623,000	627,000	622,000	644,000	658,318	702,955	704,550	709,998
Lynn	—	316,000	317,000	312,000	326,000	331,866	355,028	355,907	359,748
Springfield	461,000	433,000	424,000	418,000	426,000	445,162	481,793	471,919	474,123
Worcester	369,000	348,000	354,000	349,000	368,000	377,385	408,282	401,707	405,261
Maryland State Program	345,000	335,000	348,000	345,000	357,000	362,346	401,808	399,689	409,020
Baltimore	7,936,000	7,754,000	7,649,000	8,038,000	8,195,000	8,657,224	10,043,043	8,887,872	9,038,879
Frederick[e]	535,000	518,000	524,000	539,000	575,000	603,776	977,937	823,714	707,425
Michigan State Program	911,000	862,000	877,000	893,000	941,000	980,158	1,056,103	1,051,579	1,064,798
Detroit	1,979,000	1,554,000	1,597,000	1,640,000	1,979,000	2,066,997	1,944,506	2,016,944	2,200,845

MSA, State, or Territory	FY2004	FY2005	FY2006	FY2007	FY2008	FY2009	FY2010	FY2011	FY2012
Warren	405,000	392,000	397,000	409,000	437,000	456,391	498,501	495,727	504,993
Minnesota State Program	110,000	105,000	112,000	114,000	119,000	124,525	137,625	139,821	142,672
Minneapolis	839,000	797,000	829,000	833,000	873,000	903,558	977,370	1,006,587	1,019,484
Missouri State Program	496,000	475,000	455,000	450,000	473,000	492,485	526,694	531,035	532,894
Kansas City	978,000	924,000	918,000	918,000	955,000	1,016,453	1,108,522	1,110,292	1,115,258
St. Louis	1,217,000	1,158,000	1,150,000	1,140,000	1,227,000	1,264,901	1,362,053	1,375,810	1,394,864
Mississippi State Program	756,000	749,000	778,000	783,000	833,000	858,039	948,759	951,304	977,731
Jackson	724,000	998,000	868,000	899,000	885,000	881,503	970,233	982,379	1,147,882
North Carolina Program	2,082,000	2,010,000	2,097,000	2,154,000	2,272,000	2,387,029	2,685,680	2,397,730	2,445,019
Charlotte	571,000	565,000	597,000	626,000	671,000	714,063	793,382	813,905	830,903
Greensboro	—	—	—	—	—	—	—	309,502	316,214
Wake County	352,000	337,000	366,000	382,000	434,000	459,800	721,566	678,603	670,467
Nebraska State Program	—	—	—	—	306,000	317,829	344,586	348,643	358,165
New Jersey State Program[b]	1,106,000	1,050,000	1,064,000	1,056,000	1,079,000	1,109,696	1,180,213	1,178,084	1,184,121
Camden	657,000	628,000	620,000	610,000	642,000	655,912	713,814	711,612	719,694
Jersey City	—	2,240,000	2,545,000	2,443,000	2,534,087	2,358,602	2,926,790	2,920,338	3,002,370
Newark	5,182,000	5,014,000	5,246,000	4,924,000	5,167,000	4,913,428	6,620,013	6,646,588	7,218,919
Paterson	—	1,265,000	1,282,000	1,250,000	1,286,736	1,301,766	1,404,206	1,381,032	1,380,000
Woodbridge/Edison[f]	1,462,000	1,366,000	1,375,000	1,351,000	1,390,000	1,408,877	1,516,177	1,497,875	1,497,762
New Mexico State Program	533,000	503,000	514,000	514,000	532,000	552,442	272,536	280,246	281,585
Albuquerque[g]	—	—	—	—	—	—	320,778	324,634	326,702

MSA, State, or Territory	FY2004	FY2005	FY2006	FY2007	FY2008	FY2009	FY2010	FY2011	FY2012
Nevada State Program	238,000	219,000	219,000	219,000	228,000	236,818	254,785	255,631	255,069
Las Vegas	916,000	886,000	882,000	897,000	952,000	1,002,015	1,098,706	1,105,651	1,122,382
New York State Program	1,776,000	1,702,000	1,797,000	1,809,000	1,897,000	1,938,459	2,139,773	2,154,810	2,098,332
Albany	429,000	415,000	436,000	439,000	462,000	471,430	508,525	508,035	500,639
Buffalo	472,000	456,000	480,000	480,000	507,000	521,962	565,329	567,151	550,703
Islip	1,660,000	1,565,000	1,617,000	1,608,000	1,675,000	1,711,266	1,848,859	1,836,229	1,789,637
New York City	60,355,000	47,056,000	56,610,000	54,723,000	56,811,177	52,654,359	54,718,998	55,968,315	54,245,344
Poughkeepsie	604,000	577,000	679,000	812,000	947,000	655,310	702,119	698,901	672,598
Rochester	597,000	575,000	599,000	605,000	640,000	658,519	709,220	713,226	691,595
Ohio State Program	1,041,000	1,024,000	1,037,000	1,051,000	1,108,000	1,157,420	1,249,280	1,264,841	1,274,948
Cincinnati	550,000	517,000	518,000	530,000	562,000	584,124	643,644	657,741	672,796
Cleveland	854,000	822,000	826,000	840,000	870,000	895,337	960,454	963,208	967,243
Columbus	584,000	584,000	596,000	608,000	641,000	667,342	735,952	768,105	793,899
Oklahoma State Program	518,000	494,000	498,000	506,000	226,000	230,000	243,925	247,359	246,560
Oklahoma City	466,000	441,000	435,000	437,000	459,000	483,261	513,746	519,333	519,042
Tulsa	—	—	—	—	307,000	324,647	342,706	349,450	349,062
Oregon State Program	—	321,000	319,000	317,000	335,000	350,114	374,867	376,285	378,349
Portland	1,006,000	949,000	947,000	943,000	988,000	1,016,854	1,088,055	1,086,484	1,090,721
Pennsylvania State Program	1,540,000	1,511,000	1,548,000	1,527,000	1,670,000	1,755,180	1,615,167	1,600,168	1,615,304
Allentown[h]	—	—	—	—	—	—	317,228	322,414	324,921
Philadelphia	7,632,000	7,336,000	7,083,000	6,650,000	7,052,000	8,716,376	8,786,271	7,385,176	7,701,943
Pittsburgh	626,000	620,000	623,000	619,000	649,000	676,967	731,148	729,568	731,171

MSA, State, or Territory	FY2004	FY2005	FY2006	FY2007	FY2008	FY2009	FY2010	FY2011	FY2012
Puerto Rico State Program	1,748,000	1,636,000	1,633,000	1,616,000	1,679,000	1,709,461	1,825,260	1,806,368	1,810,019
San Juan	7,140,000	5,324,000	5,874,000	5,632,000	6,144,000	6,266,967	6,430,001	6,312,892	5,882,407
Providence	807,000	764,000	776,000	773,000	801,000	820,541	874,203	872,012	877,009
South Carolina State Program	1,387,000	1,356,000	1,387,000	1,403,000	1,491,000	1,563,881	1,708,727	1,728,286	1,474,412
Charleston	418,000	390,000	397,000	401,000	419,000	437,943	477,408	547,873	560,081
Columbia	1,270,000	1,160,000	1,041,000	1,034,000	1,138,000	1,404,470	1,566,258	1,540,616	1,584,363
Greenville	—	—	—	—	—	—	—	—	297,217
Tennessee State Program	739,000	718,000	747,000	756,000	796,000	830,568	911,377	916,803	947,455
Memphis	2,134,000	1,462,000	1,882,000	1,879,000	2,115,000	2,019,277	1,701,201	1,540,635	1,705,456
Nashville	737,000	840,000	737,000	757,000	795,000	829,966	903,441	911,759	900,557
Texas State Program	2,736,000	2,634,000	2,691,000	2,733,000	2,841,000	2,625,853	2,818,502	2,807,104	2,830,690
Austin	988,000	931,000	940,000	947,000	987,000	1,029,086	1,103,927	1,096,976	1,100,219
Dallas	3,192,000	3,867,000	3,141,000	3,134,000	3,332,000	3,642,608	3,722,637	3,969,841	4,060,375
El Paso	—	—	—	—	—	327,655	355,028	355,503	355,395
Fort Worth	835,000	805,000	813,000	819,000	863,000	892,529	950,848	936,172	942,706
Houston	5,068,000	9,669,000	6,039,000	6,579,000	6,038,000	7,315,504	7,793,944	7,127,183	7,572,952
San Antonio	1,027,000	960,000	971,000	972,000	1,025,000	1,064,378	1,151,125	1,168,601	1,187,881
Utah State Program	120,000	111,000	112,000	111,000	115,000	117,707	126,975	127,715	129,216
Salt Lake City	386,000	354,000	353,000	346,000	357,000	363,348	387,189	387,583	386,858
Virginia State Program	640,000	612,000	618,000	615,000	634,000	667,943	703,999	725,533	727,609
Richmond	692,000	658,000	665,000	660,000	690,000	702,433	774,169	781,825	864,491
Virginia Beach	1,022,000	958,000	941,000	937,000	968,000	1,002,215	1,079,493	1,093,344	1,089,336
Washington State Program	652,000	619,000	620,000	622,000	651,000	671,553	728,016	722,709	728,203

MSA, State, or Territory	FY2004	FY2005	FY2006	FY2007	FY2008	FY2009	FY2010	FY2011	FY2012
Seattle	1,688,000	1,611,000	1,615,000	1,604,000	1,663,000	1,705,852	1,821,710	1,809,798	1,814,768
Wisconsin State Program	405,000	383,000	389,000	391,000	407,000	422,102	455,271	460,217	463,438
Milwaukee	512,000	487,000	497,000	492,000	515,000	531,988	574,936	576,432	579,000
West Virginia State Program	—	—	—	—	—	309,608	336,232	336,134	339,564
—Subtotal formula grants	263,039,000	251,323,000	256,162,000	256,162,000	267,417,000	276,089,000	298,485,000	297,888,030	298,800,000
—Subtotal competitive grants	29,227,000	27,925,000	28,463,000	28,463,000	29,713,000	30,676,000	33,165,000	32,100,000i	33,200,000
—Subtotal technical asst.	2,485,000	2,480,000	1,485,000	1,485,000	1,485,000	1,485,000	3,350,000	3,343,000	—
Total HOPWA	294,751,000	281,728,000	286,110,000	286,110,000	300,100,000	310,000,000	335,000,000	334,330,000i	332,000,000

Source: U.S. Department of Housing and Urban Development, Office of Community Planning and Development Program Formula Allocations, http://portal.hud.gov/hudportal/HUD?src=/program_offices/comm_planning/communitydevelopment/budget, and the Office of Community Planning and Development Appropriations Budget page, http://www.hud.gov/offices/cpd/about/budget/index.cfm.

a. The State of California administers the grant for the Bakersfield and Fresno MSAs. See U.S. Department of Housing and Urban Development, *2012 HOPWA Formula Operating Instructions*, January 31, 2012, p. 4, http://www.hudhre.info/documents/2012Operating_Formula.pdf.

b. According to directions in HUD Appropriations Acts, funds awarded to the Wilmington MSA are transferred to the State of New Jersey to administer the HOPWA program for the one New Jersey county that is in the Wilmington MSA (Salem county).

c. The State of Florida administers the grants for the Cape Coral, Lakeland, Bradenton, and Palm Bay MSAs. *2012 HOPWA Formula Operating Instructions*, p. 4.

d. After FY2009, Deltona no longer qualified for funds. U.S. Department of Housing and Urban Development, *2010 HOPWA Formula Operating Instructions*, April 1, 2010, p. 1, http://www.hudhre.info/documents/2010Operating_Formula.pdf.

e. The State of Maryland administers the grant for the Bethesda-Frederick-Gaithersburg MSA. *2012 HOPWA Formula Operating Instructions*, p. 4.

f. Starting in FY2010, Edison, NJ replaced Woodbridge as the designated HOPWA grantee. *2010 HOPWA Formula Operating Instructions*, p. 1.

g. The State of New Mexico administers the grant for Albuquerque. *2012 HOPWA Formula Operating Instructions*, p. 4.

h. The State of Pennsylvania administers the grant for Allentown. *2012 HOPWA Formula Operating Instructions*, p. 4.

i. Competitive grants for FY2011 are based on HUD's announcement of the renewal of existing grants ($23 million) and the NOFA for new competitive grants ($9.1 million).

j. The FY2012 Department of Defense and Full-Year Appropriation Act (P.L. 112-10) contained an across-the-board rescission of 0.2% for all discretionary accounts. The rescission reduced the HOPWA appropriation ($335 million) by approximately $670,000.

Author Contact Information

Libby Perl
Specialist in Housing Policy
eperl@crs.loc.gov, 7-7806

www.ingramcontent.com/pod-product-compliance
Lightning Source LLC
Chambersburg PA
CBHW081417170526
45166CB00010B/3383